If Not Now, When?

If Not Now, When?

**We are never at the end of anything.
We are always at the beginning of everything!**

ELLEN NALABOFF

ISBN: 1511646136
ISBN 13: 9781511646130
Library of Congress Control Number: 2015905643
CreateSpace Independent Publishing Platform
North Charleston, South Carolina

Introduction

Every one of us has the ability to make a choice. We can either stay on the same path that we have been traveling down, regardless of the results, or we can choose to travel a different path. It takes courage to choose the latter, but I have found it is well worth the effort.

The choices we make will determine whether we live a life of frustration and disease or an extraordinary life filled with abundance and health. Choose wisely, because your life depends on it!

I have taken many different paths on my journey, and I am now setting out on a new one: the path of an author. I have chosen this path because I would love to share the accumulation of all my knowledge and thoughts with all of you.

There are so many different roads that I have taken, and I believe so many more yet to come; there's so much more to achieve and learn. As I enter into my 57th year, I feel as if life is just beginning for me and adventure waits around every bend. I would love to be able to share these feelings with everyone who feels like they are too old to move forward!

We are never at the end of anything. We are always at the beginning of everything!

"TO HEALTH AND WELLNESS!"

Table of Contents

One

If Not Now, When?

"Your time is limited, so don't waste it living some-one else's life. Don't be trapped by dogma-which is living with the results of other people's think-ing. Don't let the noise of others' opinions drown out your own inner voice. And most important, have the courage to follow your heart and intu-ition. They somehow already know what you truly want to become. Everything else is secondary."

_ STEVE JOBS, ENTREPRENEUR

There is no predetermined time for how long our journey will take and where it will take us in this lifetime. At what age do we believe we begin (or stop) moving forward? Why do we put limitations on ourselves with age? Why do so many people in this society think that when you hit middle age it's all over? So many believe if you haven't gone after those dreams or achieved the goals you set for yourself by a certain age, then it's never going to happen.

I think that's a very sad way to look at life. Contrary to this belief, I think we can achieve anything we want no matter at what age we try. The age at which this society has dictated middle age to be is 45-50. This is actually a point in your life where you can make major changes; changes which can influence both your own life and the lives of others. When you were born into this world, you were pretty much helpless and you had to depend on others for your needs to be met. As you grew, you had to learn how to crawl and to speak. Your childhood was all about learning. When you became school-aged, you had to study and prepare for tests and do countless homework assignments. There was so much placed on our shoulders, all dictated by what society expected of us.

When we finally entered our college years, we were weighed down with thoughts of our future: how we were going to make a living, what profession we would choose? For many of us, after we graduated we started working and eventually we married. We pursued careers with hopes that we could become financially independent and able to support ourselves and our family. So many women spend a good part of their 30s and 40s raising children. We try to give them the best we possibly can. We teach them, support them, nurture them and set them out on their own paths.

If Not Now, When?

Once we have accomplished these things and set them out on their journey in life, what happens to us? Where are we in our life's journey? I know quite a few women who find that this time in life is very rough. They feel lost and sad about a life not lived, dreams not fulfilled. Men go through this as well; this is what so many refer to as a midlife crisis.

We turn around, look at our lives, and ask ourselves, "What do I have? Where am I?" We say, "I never got to achieve all those dreams I imagined I would when I was younger." I remember wanting to become a writer, a great dancer, an accomplished singer, and a Broadway actor. What happened to all those dreams? They were put aside while we were busy providing for and raising a family.

I am here writing this to all of you to tell you it isn't too late. It's never too late, the time is now; this is it, and why not? You have accomplished so much already, and the future is in front of you. You've spent so much time on the things you had to do in order to arrive at this great point in your journey. This is finally your time, this is all about you. This time is a rebirth. There is nothing you have to do but follow your dreams. Now you are set free to pursue those dreams, with the power you have accumulated through knowledge and experience. You have the tools needed to follow those passions to achieve your dreams. This is it. There is no time like the present; this is the moment.

I encourage my clients, and all the men and women I meet, to stop thinking that they're too old and life has passed them by. I meet people all the time who say to me, "You know, Ellen, I'm already 40 years old. Everything is falling apart, my body, my skin; I am getting old." My response is usually one expressed with great passion. It usually goes something like this: "Old, are you kidding? Do you want to know what old is?" Old is what you believe it to be. If you choose to believe that old is 40, then you will be old at 40. I know 30-year-olds who think they're old, and I know 90-year-olds who think they're young. I believe you're old when you stop moving forward and when you stop growing; that is old. When you stop embracing life and learning something new every day, regardless of what it is, that is old. When we stop observing and paying attention, that's when we begin to age. If we are not moving forward, we are dying.

For so many of us, when we hit middle age and our children are grown, we begin to ask ourselves, "What is my purpose now, who am I, what have I accomplished with my life?" We tell ourselves, "All of those dreams I once dared to dream are behind me." When asked those questions, my answer is that it's just not true. There are still so many dreams yet to be fulfilled and challenges yet to be conquered, if you allow yourself to look at age differently. I am excited every day to wake up and to think about what new adventures await me. What can I accomplish today, what new thing can I learn, and where can I apply this knowledge?

I recently had dinner with a friend who asked me, "When is it okay to stop going to the gym, when can we stop worrying about how we look and working so hard to be fit? When can we just be done?" I looked at her and said, "Never. Why would you ever want to be done?" Every year, every day, and every moment is filled with endless possibilities. It's a chance for growth, it's a chance to make a difference, to make your life matter. "IF NOT NOW, WHEN?"

Two

In the Now, Present Time Consciousness

*"I don't control life, but I can control
how I react to it."*

-MACKLEMORE, *MUSICIAN*

We spend so much of our time mentally either in the past or in the future. We are very rarely focused in the now. We think about the past and the things we should have done or shouldn't have; we regret bad decisions we might have made; we think about things that have hurt us. We dwell in all of that negativity from the past, and it sets us up for pain and stress in the present and future. Those past regrets and pain follow us into the future because we live in them. I constantly hear people making excuses and saying, "I'll do it tomorrow. I'll go to the gym when I look better in my workout clothes." Another common excuse is "I'll save that for when my children are older and I have more time."

That's a big mistake, because life will never get easier on its own; it will never effortlessly slow down, and you will never find yourself in the perfect place all of a sudden. You have to create that place. You have to make that time, and there's no time like the present.

Change can only occur in the here and now. We can't keep looking back, because that part of our life is in the past. We can't change any of that, and it's a waste of energy to dwell there. We also cannot keep putting off everything for the future and hoping things change. The only tangible time that we have is the very moment we are in. The present is where we can make changes and choices that will affect our lives. Those changes cannot happen in the past, and we have no control over the future.

Can we let go of all those thoughts, wrapped up in both the past and future, and spend some time in the moment? How are you living this very moment that you are in? Can you slow down enough to appreciate this very second? Are you aware of your surroundings, the people you're with? Do you hear them, and are you paying attention to what they are saying? Do you see the beauty of the sky in the morning when you wake up, or the colors of the sun when it is setting? Do you stop long enough to truly listen to the people that you love? And I mean truly listen, undivided attention; or are you too occupied in your own head with everything you have to do in the future or everything you already did? If you are, you will lose the moment which is the only place where change can really happen and life can fully be lived.

Three

"Go for the moon. If you don't get it, you'll still be heading for a star. Happiness lies not in the mere possession of money; it lies in the joy of achievement, in the thrill of the creative effort."

- Franklin D. Roosevelt, U.S. President

⌒

Being present and living in the moment—how can we develop the ability to achieve that? We can start at the beginning. How you wake up in the morning, how your day begins is such an important part of how the day is going to unfold for you. There's a great saying that states, "How you live your day is how you live your life." Are you always rushing through your day impatient, anxious and stressed? Do you feel a constant churning inside telling you that you must move faster in order to get everything accomplished? Do you feel as if you're always playing the catch-up game? Moving so quickly without thought, trying to finish everything, is not a good way to live.

Maybe you are one of the few who go through their day in a very calm appreciative way, filled with joy, knowing that whatever has to be accomplished will be. I think very few people go through their days that way, however.

Here are a few tips on how you can start living your life in a gentle, more relaxed manner. When you move from a place of calm, you are able to accomplish so much more. When you wake up in the morning and open your eyes, what do you normally think about? What first runs through your head? Are your thoughts positive ones that bring you a sense of well- being, or are they negative ones loaded with stress and anxiety? The way you wake up in the morning and start your day is very important. Do you jump out of bed and fling yourself into the shower, or do you wake up calmly and slowly? It is a great idea when you first open your eyes to be still for a few moments and practice gratitude. It doesn't have to be a long time, just a few moments. Take a deep breath, and think of all the things you have to be thankful for. I like to be thankful for another day in my life. I think about the wonderful warm bed I am in and the beautiful home I live in. I give thanks for the people in my life; my family, my coworkers, my friends, my job.

Take a moment when you wake up and run through your life. Look only for the good things, the ones that make you smile and feel happy. Grab one thought (it could be a person, an event, a vacation) about some moment in time when you were filled with joy and peace, and think about that for a minute. Hold onto that thought and rise up out of bed. As you shower, instead of spending your time rushing to get out and running your 'to do' list over and over in your head, stop for a moment. Take a deep breath, and then follow that breath with another and be in the moment. Enjoy the shower. Take notice of how the warm water feels on your body, how the soap smells, see the steam rising. Be in gratitude for that wonderful shower. Focus on that instead of your 'to do' list. You already know what needs to be done, so why run it over 1,000 times in your head before you even get to any tasks? I think that is exhausting, and it can make you worn out before you even begin your day. When you step out of that shower, notice how that soft dry towel feels. Stop in front of the mirror and look at yourself and say, "You look great. I love you. We are going to have an amazing day, today's going to be filled with great things." This practice of looking at your reflection in the mirror is called *mirror work*, and it is very powerful. We will discuss it further in Chapter 5.

When we set those intentions for our day, we set the course for how the day will go. It is a way to start the day that allows us to hold onto our energy and not waste it. That energy can be used in a much more productive way than wasting it, dwelling on our 'to do' lists before even starting them. Throughout your day, take time to appreciate. While you're driving to work, look around and practice gratitude for the place you live, for the trees, the sky, and all of nature. Look for beauty and take time to notice it.

Focus on what makes you feel good rather than what makes you feel bad. Put music on while you drive and sing out loud. Avoid phone calls that have the ability to stress you; there will be plenty of time later in the day for those. Get to work in the calmest mindset that you possibly can. Smile at your coworkers and employees, and thank them from your heart for all their hard work and the help they have provided you. Acknowledge them and show them how much you appreciate them. By doing this, you will put yourself in a positive mindset. Those thoughts, smiles, and gratitude will be the energy and vibrational field that will create your day. That energy will come back to you throughout the day, in the form of how others react to you and speak to you. By treating people this way and creating that energy, you will create a powerful force field; one that will affect everyone and everything in its path.

We can also set our day up completely opposite from this, and create a day full of negative energy. If you choose to start your day in a crazy, stressed-out manner and use negative words such as, "This is going to be a crazy day, I have way too much to do today," you are setting the stage for exactly that kind of day to unfold. We all know the saying, "When it rains, it pours." Who needs negativity and crazy energy pouring down on us? Choose your words carefully! Instead of putting forth negativity, choose sentences like: "This is going to be a great day! I am going to get this job done and enjoy the process."

If Not Now, When?

Make a conscious effort to speak to people with gratitude and appreciation. Make an effort to enter every part of your day with calm energy. Try not to worry; it will all get done, one step at a time. I always tell my children, "Do not look at the final product, because when you do, the task seems overwhelming. Take it piece by piece and it will be accomplished." Stop thinking about it all at once, because the task will be daunting and you will become full of anxiety and stress. This is a total waste of energy. So much more will be accomplished if it's done step by step, calmly and in due time. It will be finished in the time it was meant to be. If you try to do 10 things at once, something will be sacrificed. Each task done well will build upon another, leading to an amazing job well done.

At the end of the day, when your day is complete and you are at home, try and maintain that energy and gratitude. When you finally lay your head down on the pillow, what runs through your head? What do you think about before you go to sleep? The thoughts that you run through your head at the end of the day are also very important. They impact how you sleep and how tomorrow will unfold. I like to lie in bed and run through my day like a short film. I think about everything from the moment I woke up to where I am at the present moment. I think about everything that transpired, the people I came in contact with, the way I treated them, and the way they treated me. I ask myself, "Could I have done anything differently? Could I have handled any situations differently?" I do not dwell on anything, I just run it through my head. I take a moment to appreciate all I have accomplished, and give thanks for another blessed day to live my life.

None of this comes easily. Like anything you want to be good at, it needs to be practiced. By practicing this, you will be able to create a more empowered life. Nothing can be done well when you are stressed and anxious. Those emotions are so negative and constricting. They will create your day, your week, your year, and ultimately your life. I don't know how you feel about this, but I chose not to live in that energy.

When you finally lay your head down on that pillow, take a moment to thank the universe and all the people in your life, and be grateful in that moment for all of it. This is a great way to end your day. Practice gratitude throughout your day, for everyone and everything you come in contact with. It is a great way to empower yourself and the people around you. Take the path of least resistance; if you journey down a path that is resisting you too much, fighting you, simply chose another path. If you do not chose a different path, you will create negative energy and that energy will clash against itself and create a stone wall. Nothing will be accomplished in that force field. Sit back and take the easier path, the one of least resistance that will get you where you need to go, and accept the people in your life for who and what they are. Enter your day with gratitude for all, and end your day the same way—in gratitude.

Four

SEIZING THE MOMENT

*"Stop letting people who do so little for you control
so much of your mind, feelings, and emotions."*

-WILL SMITH, ACTOR

$\sim$

If you want to make change, you must seize the moment. If you want to move forward and grow, keeping your excitement for life, you have to grab onto the opportunity while it is in your path. So many of us get stuck in the limiting beliefs of the society we live in. We are often held back by what people think of us, what is considered normal for our age and gender, the roles that society places upon us and what is expected of us. Whether or not someone is considered old or young at a certain age is determined by this belief system. These limiting beliefs dictate to us what we can or cannot accomplish at a certain age. This belief system dictates to many of us that at the age of 40 we have entered midlife. It's a system that makes us think that we are getting old, and we are slowing down at that age.

This is the same belief system that tells many women and men that if they have not fulfilled their dreams and desires by now, they might as well give up. For many women, it is a time when their bodies start to enter peri- menopause with all the changes connected to that cycle. I have counseled many women who are made to believe that this is a time of great decline. They fear the loss of their youth and how they will be viewed by society. These beliefs are placed upon us by society and how our culture views age and youth.

There are many cultures around the world where this belief does not exist. Instead of thinking that *as women age they lose their value and purpose*, these cultures revere women and hold them in high esteem. These women are valued for their wisdom and knowledge that can only be acquired through experience.

In American culture, we tell women that they're not expected to have energy and be beautiful as they age. It is a time when women begin to feel so bad about the loss of what society deems beautiful that they look to the medical profession to ease their pain. They put themselves through all types of cosmetic procedures to try and slow down the inevitable, holding on so tightly to beauty and youth. I would like to propose a different way of looking at the process of aging.

If Not Now, When?

The secret of being young and beautiful does not come from the outside. It dwells within—in your spirit and soul. That's where true beauty and youth comes from. If you want to stay young, full of vibrancy and energy, focus on what's within—not on the surface. It is not about the wrapping paper that surrounds the gift, but what lies underneath that matters. That is the true gift. We will all wrinkle as we age; it is an absolute. The flawless skin of youth will vanish, but we only need to look beyond this to see something far greater; the power of experience and knowledge.

I have a friend who loves to say, "As soon as you get your shit together, your ass falls apart." I love that saying. When we hit our 40s and 50s, we are in a much different mental state then we were in during our 20s. We have finally begun to trust our instincts and understand ourselves. At this age, we become much more in tune to our wants and needs. We have a better sense of self and who we are. With this knowledge comes a sense of security that is impossible to have when you're in your 20s. Girls in their 20s may think they possess this knowledge and have confidence in themselves, but how much of that is built through real growth, and how much is just ego? Maybe they feel that way because people say they're pretty or beautiful. They may be the smartest in their class or the best at a sport, but does that bring true confidence? If they do not possess the looks, the athleticism, the grades, would they still feel that way about themselves? Does this empowerment come from deep within, or is this power gained through the opinions of others?

So many young girls today think they can only empower themselves through their physical appearance. It is not that looking attractive isn't important, because it is, but it should not be the sum of who we are. We should not allow someone else's opinion of us to give us confidence or to strip us of it.

There are a lot of young women and men who do not feel very good about themselves because they are listening to the opinions of others. They are allowing the stereotypes of society to create their own belief system. Maybe they do not possess the perfect face, perfect body, or winning personality; they might not be in the cool crowd. Maybe they do not follow the normal social patterns of what an 18, 19, or 20-year-old is expected to follow. Right away they're labeled as unattractive or as losers, all because someone's beliefs and opinions say so. They can begin to view themselves this way and lose all their self-confidence. It works the other way as well; there are young men and women who possess some great attributes and spend a tremendous amount of time making sure everyone sees them. This kind of self-worth is created by other people's opinions and compliments, but is that who they really are?

How do you feel about yourself? When everyone's opinion is said and done, whether positive or negative, how do you see yourself? Can someone take you from the top of the mountain to the ground by a look, an action, or a word? If so, then your opinion of yourself is not very secure or powerful. It is the decorative wrapping paper which is so easily destroyed that you have wrapped yourself in, instead of focusing on the gift within.

In our 20s, we go through a lot of growth and sometimes pain while focused on the decorative wrapping paper that surrounds us. As we mature, hopefully we spend more time on the gift within and less on that wrapping paper. The person I thought I was in my 20s is certainly not who I am today. There may still be shadows and parts of that idea of myself within me, but it is not who I am today. We evolve, we change, and we grow. We are meant to; it's the natural process of our lives, and if we didn't that would be very sad. I'm sure all of us know people who have never grown, who are still stuck in their 20s and have never bothered to look underneath all that wrapping paper. Most are very sad and unfulfilled.

When you finally hit your 40s, you can enter it running and feeling this incredible sense of freedom. Or, you can be paralyzed in fear with thoughts of what do I do now, what is my path, who am I? Many of us have spent so much time raising a family and giving to everyone else that we forgot to spend time with ourselves. I do encourage all young girls out there who might be reading this to spend time on what makes you special, what makes you shine. It doesn't matter what other people think—this doesn't make you special; only what you believe does. Spend time with that and try to figure out your own special uniqueness. What is your purpose here? What qualities do you possess that make you special, and how can you use those gifts to enrich not only your own life, but also the lives of others?

When we are young, we have the tendency to think everything revolves around us. I would love to encourage young women to start to change that belief. It isn't about what society expects from us, and it isn't about what our peers think of us, but rather how we see ourselves that really matters. How are we special, who are we really? I know that's difficult to grasp at a young age, but that's the beauty of aging. Why not start thinking about this when you are young? More time should be spent on the quest for self-knowledge, and less on how to accumulate wealth and material things. I think this fascination with materialism is a destructive way of thinking, and ultimately one that will not allow us to find our passion.

A better approach would be to find the uniqueness that is your true gift, what you're passionate about. Once you start to get in touch with that, regardless of your age, you will find abundance in that knowledge. The Universe will support you in that quest, and you will be able to achieve great success by following your passions. This will bring you great joy if you keep on the path—regardless of what people may or may not think.

Many people have been put down and criticized for their passions and dreams. They're often told not to bother pursuing them, because so few have ever achieved them. That is a very negative outlook and it doesn't reinforce growth or change. If you have a passion for any area of life and you feel that passion down deep in your soul, you must pursue it, regardless of the opinions of others. That passion will take you on a journey which will bring you joy, enlightenment, and abundance. There is no age that this journey has to begin by or be accomplished by. The journey can begin in our 40s and 50s, or at any age. So many of us do, at this age, have a better understanding of ourselves; one that we may not have had at a younger age.

So the big question is what do we do about it? Are we afraid of it, fearful of the 'what ifs' in life? Age can make people fearful; the feelings of invincibility that we had when we were young have been replaced by doubt. Maybe you have been knocked down one too many times and it's hard to get up. Try to look at every knock down as a lesson. Your choice is to decide whether these lessons will keep you in a state of pain and fear—or if they cause you to look at situations differently and encourage you to choose a different path. That's how you have to look at those knock downs to make progress. If we didn't have those falls, we would continue down the same path and we would never journey into other directions.

Inevitably, the chances of having these setbacks are great. But these setbacks should not be allowed to drain our passion—but instead, should actually serve to wake us up and redirect us down a new path. What are the joys and pleasures awaiting us on this new path? Do not allow fear and doubt to stop you from moving forward. Follow those passions and those dreams. There is so much abundance out there, and so much to learn and achieve. We are just at the beginning of our journey. We have had just a glimpse of the road when we hit middle-age. We need to walk down the rest of that road, or better yet, we should run!

Five

*"When you learn to harness the power of your fears,
it can take you places beyond your wildest dreams."*

- JIMMY LOVINE, MUSIC PRODUCER

Mirror work is a powerful way of empowering oneself. What exactly is mirror work, and how does it help?

Every morning when you wake up, get out of bed, and go into the bathroom, what do you see? Do you see your reflection in the mirror? When you see that reflection, what is your reaction to it? Does it bring you joy, or does it make you unhappy? I would like you to start a practice of looking into the mirror and saying hello to yourself. Not just hello but words like, "Hello beautiful, you are amazing. I love you."

Yes, I know that may sound a bit crazy and even crazier when you say it out loud, but the power of those words is beyond measure.

When I initially give this assignment to my clients, they react in one of two ways: either they laugh nervously and hope I'm kidding, or they are horrified! It's so hard for people to truly look at themselves free of judgment. Most people are extremely hard on themselves, and are not happy with the reflection they see. I say, "Do it anyway." Stand in front of that mirror and look deep into your own eyes and tell that beautiful soul within how much you love it. It's important to say the words out loud and with commitment. Smile at yourself and say the words "I am amazing."

At first these words will probably be difficult to say, but say them anyway. The more you practice saying this out loud, the easier it will become. The easier it becomes, the more you will believe these statements—and the more you believe them, the more self-worth you will have. If you cannot look deep into your own eyes and say these words, how can you ever expect anyone else to? If you do not 'own' the beliefs, no one else will believe you're amazing either. It all starts with you. Look into that mirror and find everything that is great about you, and allow that to be the voice with the power. Sometimes we can even make someone else feel that positive energy as well. I remember one time saying out loud in the bathroom, "You are fantastic and so beautiful." Then I heard my husband say from outside the door, "Thank you." He thought I was speaking to him, and it made him feel good. Two people benefited from this practice, how great! Start this practice today. "If not now, when?"

Six

*"A man is a success if he gets up in the morning
and gets to bed at night, and in between
he does what he wants to do."*

-Bob Dylan, musician

One way to achieve optimal health and to cultivate enough energy to live a great life is to get enough sleep. Sleep is so critical to the health of both your body and mind. Most people require 7 to 8 hours of sleep per night. We are all tuned into the natural rhythms of daily and seasonal light. The cycles of light and dark that result from the movement of the moon and sun affect all living creatures. We are no exception to this natural law. Our physiology is the same as our ancient sun-driven ancestors. The problem we face is that we are in the age of technology and we have the availability of artificial light 24 hours a day. Late-night TV and bright lights at the touch of a switch make it easy to forget the thousands of years that we lived in sync with the cycles of day and night.

As the sun rises, things begin to occur chemically within our bodies. Our hormones shift in response to the rising of the sun. Whenever light stimulates your skin or eyes, regardless of the source, your brain and hormonal system react as if it is morning. In response to this light, your hormonal system releases cortisol. This hormone is an activating hormone that is released in times of stress. It activates the body and prepares it for movement. Light is a form of electromagnetic stress, which gets the systems of the body ready for work, combat, or whatever is necessary for survival. As the sun rises, our cortisol levels also begin to rise. They peak between 6 a.m. and 9 a.m. Then they drop a little, but remain high through midday, supporting daily activities. In the afternoon cortisol levels drop significantly, especially as the sun goes down. Decreasing cortisol levels allows the release of the hormone melatonin, as well as an increase in our growth and repair hormones. If we follow our natural sleep and wake cycles, we will start to wind down as the sun sets in preparation for sleep. Physical repair happens while we sleep between the hours of 10 p.m. and 2 a.m. From the hours of 2 a.m. through waking, the immune and repair systems of the body focus on the mental and nervous systems.

Our brightly lit houses, late-night TV, and working late into the evening will keep the levels of stress hormones high way past sundown. Florescent lights, TVs, and computer screens flicker on and off between 60 and 120 cycles per session, which your brain interprets as the morning sun. Cortisol can take hours to clear from your blood stream, which will prevent the normal release of melatonin, growth hormones, and important immune factors. This will cut into your immune system's valuable repair time. If you go to bed after midnight, you have already missed over two hours of your physical repair cycle, which starts at 10 p.m. People who work the graveyard shift or parents waking up at irregular times have their mental repair cycle interrupted. These people usually have a long list of nagging muscular and skeletal injuries. They can suffer from an increase in headaches, a loss of energy, depression, anxiety and even neurological disorders. If you do not get sufficient sleep at night, you cannot possibly have energy when you wake.

Getting a good night's sleep is critical to health and vitality. It keeps your immune system strong and able to fight off infections. It also helps in the maintenance of your metabolism. People who do not sleep well at night usually have a slow metabolism. Getting enough sleep is critical to weight management. The health of your cardiovascular system is also determined by how much sleep you are getting. Learning and memory also can be affected by the quality and quantity of sleep. Sleep helps the brain commit new information to memory through a process called memory consolidation. People who sleep after learning a new task do better on the test later. If you are a student studying for a test, instead of pulling an all-nighter, go to sleep. Sleep will help process that information and put it to memory.

Our metabolism and our weight are affected by the amount of quality sleep we get. Sleep helps determine how our body processes and stores carbohydrates—by altering levels of hormones like cortisol. This can effect both our appetite and our weight. If we do not get enough sleep, we may be irritable and moody. Loss of sleep will also have an effect on our ability to concentrate. Lack of sleep can also leave you too tired to accomplish the things you want to do. How can you move forward in your life and keep growing, if you're always tired?

Cardiovascular problems, such as hypertension, irregular heartbeat, and increased stress levels, have been linked to sleep deprivation. Lack of sleep will weaken our immune system, which will result in our bodies' inability to fight off disease.

How do we achieve a good night's sleep? Start by putting away your laptop, get off Facebook, and turn your phone off. You want to calm down at the end of the day and relax. Relaxation will help to calm down your brain. Try taking a hot bath, reading a good book, or listening to some soothing music. Shut the TV off; watching movies or shows that are very depressing or violent can result in a loss of sleep and possibly nightmares. Commit to going to sleep early. If you haven't completed all your tasks by early evening, put them off until the next day. A job well done will be accomplished when you are well rested and focused.

The food you eat and what you drink will also have an effect on your ability to get a good night sleep. Consuming alcohol at night can cause interrupted sleep. You may fall asleep quickly and easily after drinking, but most likely, you will wake up a few hours later and you probably won't dream very much—if at all. Drinking coffee late in the afternoon will also interrupt your sleep. Caffeine stays in your bloodstream for a very long period of time. If you're consuming caffeine after 3 o'clock in the afternoon, you're going to have it in your bloodstream when it is time to go to sleep.

Eating a large meal before you go to sleep will also affect the quality of your sleep. You need at least four hours to digest that meal before you put your head on the pillow. I recommend eating lightly at night. Remember to shut off your lights; all light will stimulate your body, regardless of the source. Your room should be pitch black to avoid the stimulation of cortisol. Do not leave the TV on when you fall asleep. Many people fall asleep while watching TV and leave the TV on, which will undoubtedly wake you up at some point in the evening. You may fall asleep but it will not be a deep REM sleep. Your body needs that deep, healing REM sleep. Drinking water throughout the day is a wonderful thing to do for your body, but you should stop consuming liquids after 6 p.m. Too much liquid in your system will result in a full bladder which you will have to wake up to empty at some point during the night. So if you want to get a good night's sleep, do the following:

1. Turn your lights off.
2. Eat earlier.
3. Eat a lighter evening meal.
4. Avoid stimulants like coffee and alcohol.
5. Prepare for sleep by calming down. Put away the computer and turn off the TV.

If you want to have an amazing life and have all the energy you need to accomplish this, go to sleep.

Seven

It Can Wait

"The secret is to have a sense of yourself,
your real self, your unique self. And not
just once in a while, or once a day, but all
through the day, the week and life."

-*Bill Murray, actor and comedian*

The world we live in is a very busy one, filled with lots of activity and a great deal of stress. Because of all this stress, we need to put time aside for ourselves to relax. We need to find some stillness and quiet. More and more people are suffering from exhaustion and stress. When stress and exhaustion are not acknowledged and dealt with, anxiety and depression soon follow. Everyone is complaining about having way too much to do and far too little time to do it in. It's as if time is just flying by, and we have no ability to slow down. The process of slowing down and finding balance in our hectic lives is easier said than done.

How do we slow down and find that balance? There are many ways to accomplish stillness, but one of the most effective is through meditation. I know the thought of meditating is very daunting for many. A lot of my clients tell me that it is impossible for them to meditate. This is because they have no time and way too much chatter going on in their heads. I can understand that, because I was one of those people many years ago. It takes practice and commitment, like anything else you want to accomplish. The mind is a muscle and you have to train it like any other muscle in your body. You wouldn't expect to get rocking abs from one sit up, and you can't train the mind in one attempt. The beauty of meditating is you cannot fail at it. The only failure comes from not trying.

To begin meditating, find a comfortable place where you can sit quietly without interruption. This can be difficult to find but it is out there somewhere. Once you have found this spot, shut off your phone and your computer. Disconnect anything that will interrupt you. If you have children, do this after they go to school, or if they're very young, do it while they are still sleeping. If you have a dog, make sure he does not need to go for a walk. Turn your answering machine on and begin. I think 15 minutes when you first start is a good amount of time. How do you know when 15 minutes begins and ends?

If Not Now, When?

There are many free meditation apps for smartphones you can use for setting a chime to go off at the beginning and end of each session.

Close your eyes and start to focus on your breath. Pay attention to each inhale and exhale. For beginners who have not yet received their primordial sound mantra from me, I offer the mantra of So Hum. As you inhale say the word SO quietly to yourself, and as you exhale say the word HUM. Continue with this focus, SO as you breathe in, HUM as you breathe out. There will be thoughts flowing through your mind and interrupting this pattern. Acknowledge those thoughts and release them, returning always to the breath. When you first start this practice, the thoughts will be many. With practice, you will begin to reduce the number of thoughts and begin to experience stillness. This is where the magic happens; not with the thoughts but in the space between them, in the stillness.

The advantages of meditation are well-documented and numerous. The benefits are both physical and psychological. Some of these are decreased heart rate, normalization of blood pressure, quieter breathing, reduction of stress hormones, and the strengthening of the immune system, to name just a few. It is well worth the time and commitment. Start meditating today and watch your life change. "IF NOT NOW, WHEN?"

Eight

"Don't bother just to be better than your
contemporaries or predecessors.
Try to be better than yourself."

-WILLIAM FAULKNER, WRITER

⌒

How we eat, the way we look at food, the way we think about food will determine how we feel. Food makes us who we are in more ways than you can imagine. You are what you eat. I would like everyone to think about that for a moment. Stop what you are doing and just allow that statement to resonate in you for a minute. You are made up of the food you eat. There is nothing else that provides the nourishment for your cells, your hormonal system, your skin and hair, but the food you eat. Why is it that people are so disconnected from the food they eat and the value of it? Everything you put in your mouth has a direct effect on both your mental and physical state. I frequently ask my clients, "What would you like your skin to be nourished by—a ripe, sweet avocado or a bag of potato chips?" All the processed foods, sugars, salt, deli meats, chemicals, chips, all those toxins are going into your body and they will determine the quality of your hair, skin, eyes, and breath as well as your emotions.

When people come to me and voice their concerns about how tired they are, their lack of energy, how poorly they sleep, how they are often anxious and depressed, I ask one question: "What are you eating?" The answer to this question provides many solutions to their problems. We pay more attention to the quality of the gasoline we put in our cars than the fuel we put in our bodies. If you're fortunate enough to be driving a Porsche or a Ferrari, would you ever put low-grade gasoline in that engine? The answer is no, because you value that car and how it performs. So allow me to bring the obvious to light; why do we not care enough about our own bodies to do the same? Why do we place more value on material objects than the most valuable possession we have, our own bodies? There is nothing more valuable in our lives than the body we are walking around with. Without that body, we would have no life. Without health there is no joy. If you have all the things money can buy, but you don't have your health and you don't have the energy to enjoy all those things, you are not rich at all. We need to start paying more attention to this precious treasure.

If Not Now, When?

Our souls, the very essence of who we are, are encapsulated in our bodies. The body is the vessel for spirit and soul. We would never walk into any house of worship and throw trash on the floor; we have way too much respect to do that to something that is so sacred. Yet we do that every day to our bodies when we fill our stomachs with unhealthy processed foods loaded with salts and saturated fats. Aren't we showing tremendous disrespect for ourselves and the people around us? Our bodies are shrines and they should be respected and valued as such. So next time you put food in your mouth, think about this: how much do you respect yourself? If you don't respect yourself, go right ahead and eat those unhealthy foods.

When you make those unhealthy choices, that is exactly what you are telling, not only yourself—but your family and children as well. When we bring children into the world, we have a responsibility to nourish and feed them. What are you feeding your children? There are so many excuses created for why we can't make healthy choices. A few of them that I hear quite frequently are: I'm too busy, I spend so much time running around doing after-school activities, running from one sports practice to another. Always running around leaves very little time to cook meals so we grab a quick fix, a slice of pizza or something from a fast food drive-through. At that point, it's time to ask yourself some very important questions. Better choices have to be made and our priorities reset. What is more important, getting your child to that second after-school activity (you know, the one that happens at dinner time) or the gift of health and happiness? I believe it is health and happiness. Maybe instead of having to choose, we can plan ahead and do both.

Five-year-olds cannot go grocery shopping and buy all those snacks that line so many cupboards of many kitchens in America; that is something we do. How many times have you heard someone say that their child doesn't like anything else, that this is the only thing they'll eat? My response to this statement is usually one of amazement and I ask a simple question, "Who bought that food, who went to the grocery store?" It certainly wasn't your five-year-old. You bought it and then proceeded to place the blame on the child for wanting it. Take responsibility for the poor choices your children may make when it comes to food. My dad told me a long time ago that it is a lot easier to say yes than it is to say no to a child. 'No' can bring about a tremendous amount of confrontation and stress. Saying no to a child that wants to make poor food choices can create temper tantrums and animosity. You may hear the words "I won't eat, I'm not eating that, you can't make me eat that." No child ever starved himself to death because he wouldn't eat his or her vegetables or the food you made for dinner. They may rebel and not eat that night or the next, but eventually they will get hungry and eat.

Please take care of those children; feed them well. You may think feeding them what they want makes everyone's life easier, but it doesn't. When that child can't focus and sit still in a classroom, your life and theirs will suffer. If you are receiving constant phone calls from your child's teacher explaining how they are disruptive and hyperactive during class, you have to ask the question: why? Those very same children can become depressed and suffer from anxiety. I believe so many of these situations can be avoided by making better choices with the foods they eat. The arguments that you may have for a few days over the food is well worth it—to avoid the heartache you may have for a much longer period of time. Nourish your children and family well.

The next few chapters will focus on your food choices, but understand there is a trickle-down effect. The choices you make will eventually affect everyone you love and care for. This will create a much happier environment, and you can rest assured that you are doing everything possible to provide for them a healthy, wonderful life. We can begin by acknowledging that we have a responsibility to ourselves, our bodies, the environment, and our children to make healthy choices. We are connected to everyone and everything, so choose wisely and do it now.

Nine

THE ART OF EATING

"You just need to figure out what's in your
control and what isn't and be okay with it."

-SANTIGOLD, *MUSICIAN*

The big question facing so many of us today is what foods are good to eat and what foods are not? What does a healthy breakfast look like, or a healthy lunch or dinner? The way we eat is a good place to start. The majority of Americans eat like the food pyramid. Americans very often skip breakfast or have a banana or cup of coffee. When lunch arrives, they have some quick salad or a protein bar, usually on the run. Most of our daily caloric intake happens between 4 o'clock p.m. and 10 p.m. We usually have a very large dinner and eat it late in the evening, and we snack after that. By eating this way, our bodies begin to resemble the food pyramid. We are light on top, bigger in the middle and large on the bottom. Our minds are foggy and we quite often find it hard to focus. Our waistlines grow larger and our bottoms carry most of the weight. The questions are: how do we switch that around, and what is a healthier way to eat?

If, like so many people, you lack energy during the day and find it hard to wake up, you must look to when you are eating. If you're consuming the majority of your calories after 4 p.m., of course you're going to be tired during the day. Most people find that they crash in the late afternoon. That is because not enough nutritious food was consumed in the earlier part of the day to sustain your energy late into the afternoon. We need to look at how we fuel ourselves through the day, so we can have the energy we need in the afternoon. We can begin doing this by consuming the majority of our daily caloric intake by 2:30 p.m. From 2:30 p.m. until we go to sleep, we should eat light. We should begin with a breakfast substantial enough to sustain us until lunch time, and then have a great healthy lunch with no snacking in between.

I do not believe in snacking, and I absolutely do not agree with the common practice of consuming six small meals a day. I know a lot of people believe that it keeps the blood sugars level, but it also keeps the body in a constant state of digestion. Digestion is a very big job for our bodies and requires a lot of energy to complete. When we eat all day long, we keep the body in a constant state of digestion—which actually depletes the body of energy. It's like filling up your gas tank with fuel when the tank is already full and allowing it to run out all over your car. First you must burn up the gas already in your tank before you put more in. The same can be said about food and overeating. If you eat a good breakfast, you do not need to eat again until lunch. It isn't like you're going for hours and hours between meals. Most people are not even hungry and are just snacking out of habit. If you are hungry a short time after breakfast, you must ask yourself if the breakfast was insufficient.

Ten

RISE AND DINE

*"Obstacles don't have to stop you. If you run into
a wall, don't turn around and give up. Figure out
how to climb it, go through it, or work around it."*

- MICHAEL JORDAN, BASKETBALL PLAYER

What is a good breakfast? In this chapter we will discuss what can be considered a healthy breakfast. We should try to eat breakfast around the same time every morning. One good choice for breakfast is organic eggs prepared any way you like. Two eggs with the yolks will provide all eight essential amino acids. Please do not separate the egg whites from the yolks. Having an egg white omelet is a waste of the most nutritious part of the egg, the yolk. The egg yolk contains 90% of an egg's calcium, 93% of its iron, and the yolk is one of only a handful of foods in which vitamin D is naturally found. The egg is one of nature's most perfect foods. I believe in whole foods and eating them exactly how nature provided them. When you separate the eggs, they are no longer a whole food.

There are so many ways to prepare eggs. I like scrambling them in a little coconut oil, which is a very healthy fat, or some organic butter from grass-fed cows. I season them with sea salt, black pepper, and sometimes a little turmeric, which is a wonderful spice. Turmeric helps bring down inflammation and is considered a 'superfood.' I also like to have greens with my eggs. Many stores sell greens already pre-washed, organic and packaged. I like Swiss chard, arugula, baby spinach, micro-greens or sprouts. There is very little work involved to prepare these greens besides opening the container. Make a little salad on the side with the eggs. Add a few organic cherry tomatoes and drizzle all of it with a high quality olive oil or Udo's oil, which is an organic oil made from flax, sesame, and sunflower seeds. Now you have a beautiful looking breakfast and a very healthy one.

If you choose to have coffee, have it with breakfast or right after breakfast, not first thing in the morning on an empty stomach. The reason is because coffee is very acidic and not something you want to put in an empty stomach, especially if you suffer from heartburn or acid reflux. The coffee will definitely aggravate these conditions. We need to start the day with healthy fats and nutritious foods. When you do drink your coffee, make sure you are not putting artificial sweeteners and flavored creamers in it. There are so many negative side effects from consuming artificial sweeteners; it is very important to remove them from your diet. If you need to have some kind of sweetener in your coffee, go with Stevia. Stevia is very sweet; you only need to use a drop or two. It is the only sweetener that does not raise your insulin levels. If you do not like the taste of Stevia, try a small amount of raw honey or agave nectar. If you can't find any of these, then plain raw organic sugar would be better than artificial sweeteners, with the goal being to eliminate all sweeteners.

Steam a bunch of greens the night before—it could be kale, mustard greens, or beet greens—and place them in containers in your refrigerator ready to use the next morning. Whatever I don't eat for dinner, I save in glass containers to be used the next day. I always buy the pre-diced peppers and onions, which are delicious when sautéed in coconut oil. I cook them while making my eggs and then throw them into the eggs for a great omelet. If you do not like eggs, there are many other choices available for breakfast that are very healthy. We do not have to eat what is considered by the food industry to be 'breakfast foods.' You can eat chicken, fish or grass-fed beef for breakfast; these are also healthy choices.

Forget about box cereals; 99% of them are unhealthy. Even when the box says 'heart healthy' and 'natural,' most are usually very highly processed foods. Most grains have a very high glycemic rate. Those grains will convert to sugar in your body and spike your insulin levels. I find that most women eating grains tend to put on weight. I recommend avoiding all cold cereals, including granola, even the so-called healthy ones. They usually have dried fruit which is high in sugar and added sweeteners, such as honey or maple syrup. Whenever I mention this to my clients, the next question I am asked is: what about oatmeal? Oatmeal is okay for some people and they will feel fine after eating it; but for many, that is not the case. The oats are a grain that has a high glycemic rate. After eating them, many people can get really sleepy. This is not true for everyone, so you must pay attention to how your body reacts to certain foods. Oatmeal does have many nutritional benefits, and if you tolerate grains well, this one is a good choice. If you do make oatmeal, make sure it is not instant or microwavable, or flavored; that's just candy disguised as oats. The five-minute (or longer) cooking time oatmeal is best. Buy real raw oats. Cook ½ a cup of oats in 1 cup of water and bring to a boil, then reduce the heat and cover. While it is cooking, you can be getting dressed for work. When it is ready add a little almond, hemp, or coconut milk. You can also add a dash of cinnamon, which is a natural fat burner and very healthy for you. I then would want to add some fat to it. I do that by adding in a teaspoon of flaxseed or hemp seeds or both. These are high in omega-3 fatty acids, which are healthy fats. You could also add a little coconut oil. I also would put in some nuts, maybe four or five almonds or walnuts.

You can also chose fruit for breakfast. A lot of people grab a banana to start their day, but they are very high in sugar and will spike those insulin levels way too fast; so will mangoes and pineapples. All of these fruits are very high in sugar, so eat them only once in a while. Berries have so many positive effects on your health that I would recommend choosing them over other fruits. A third of a cup is all you need, and always make sure they are organic.

If you're a big yogurt lover, and I know many who are, I suggest buying only organic whole milk plain yogurt. If you have issues with dairy, and many people do, I would use coconut milk-based or goat milk-based yogurt. All of these should be plain without any added fruit or flavoring. A strawberry or blueberry flavored yogurt has about 26 grams of sugar in it, which is like eating candy. Buy your yogurt plain and you can add fresh berries to it. I also would add some flaxseed, hemp seeds, and/or chia seeds and a handful of nuts. Again, stay away from granola; even the healthiest of them are loaded with sugar and fat. Usually the granola has nuts in it which are often roasted, and that process denatures the healthy oils of the nuts. As soon as you heat a nut to that kind of temperature, you are going to denature the oil in that nut and turn it into a free radical in your body. That is one of the reasons I tell everyone to only buy raw organic nuts. No roasted nuts, stay clear of them; nut oils are extremely susceptible to high temperatures.

Another good choice for breakfast is chia seeds. Take 2 tablespoons of chia seeds, place them in a bowl and add warm milk, coconut, hemp, or almond milk and a dash of cinnamon. Allow this mixture to sit for a few minutes and watch those chia seeds grow to nine times their original size. The seeds become the size of tapioca and have a pudding-like texture. Chia seeds are very high in omega-three fatty acids and are considered a superfood. I would add some berries and nuts to this as well.

I personally stay away from bread, but if you're going to eat it, make sure it is organic sprouted whole grain bread. In order to eat well, you must become a food detective and read the labels carefully. Do not buy food just because the labeling shows a healthy picture or uses words like 'all natural' or 'good for you.' Many times, a package of bread will say whole-grain. But, when you actually look at the label, you see that only one of the grains is a whole grain and the rest are not; the same thing goes for labels using the word 'organic.' It takes some time to read through all the ingredients, but it is definitely worth the effort it takes.

I also recommend green tea over coffee. Green tea has a lot of great health benefits. Protein shakes are another option for breakfast. If you choose to go this route, make sure your shakes are not highly processed and are made from whole foods. Find the ones that are high in protein and low in sugar. Mix it up and use different shakes; you might use hemp protein as the base one day and whey protein another. If you are using whey, make sure it is from organic grass-fed cows. I always use coconut water for my base and 1 teaspoon of coconut oil in all my mixes; that way I will be getting some healthy fat in my shake.

Eleven

What's in Your Lunch Box?

*"You must do the thing you
think you cannot do."*

- *Eleanor Roosevelt, humanitarian*

⟿

L unch should be eaten somewhere between four and five hours after breakfast. Between breakfast and lunch, you should be drinking lots of water. I think if you eat a complete breakfast—one that consists of a complex carbohydrate, a healthy fat, and protein—you will be able to get through your morning without snacking. If that is just not happening for you, and you feel tired and very hungry, then go for that snack. However, make absolutely certain that you are actually hungry and really need that snack—that you're not just eating out of habit. One of my favorite snacks is an organic apple. I also like crudité with a little hummus or guacamole. Make sure if you are eating these dips that you keep it to one tablespoon of either. Take a tablespoon out of the container and put the container away to avoid overeating. You want to eat just enough to take that edge off your hunger and not to fill you up. The snack is just a little something to hold you over to your next meal. We do not need to eat unless we are hungry. Make sure you have burned through all the food that was eaten for breakfast before you begin to refuel.

I like my lunch to be my biggest meal of the day. I eat a big lunch and breakfast. Most of my physical activity happens in the morning, which makes me really hungry when lunch time rolls around. By lunchtime I have burned up all my fuel from breakfast. I drink a lot of water between breakfast and lunch, and quite often I will have a green juice. The green juice I drink is only greens, no fruit. When you exercise a lot, you build up acidity in your body and anything green helps turn your body back into an alkaline state. I also use powdered chlorella, which is a form of chlorophyll, and mix that in my water after my workouts. When you exercise, the body produces lactic acid, and by drinking green juices we will minimize the effect of that acid on the body and bring the body back to a neutral pH level. You can also do this by adding lemon to your water.

Lunch quite often consists of leftovers from the previous night's dinner. When you cook dinner, it is a good habit to get into preparing for more people than are actually eating that night. This way you always have leftovers. Say that I had prepared wild Salmon for dinner the night before, and I have enough left over for lunch. I would take that Salmon and put it over a bed of greens, add some cherry tomatoes, maybe some roasted veggies, and/or raw peppers. I might also add some raw pistachio nuts for a little crunch, and always a good quality olive oil, sea salt and pepper. I always have a form of protein for lunch and for me that protein comes from an animal source, but you can also do it with plant proteins. Having protein at lunch really revs up your engine and satisfies your hunger. We need all eight essential amino acids and those are easily found in all fish, poultry and meats. Eggs are another good choice for lunch as long as you did not have them for breakfast. Soup is also great for lunch, but make sure you always add some kind of protein.

I personally do not eat bread, but if I want to have something that resembles a wrap I might use collard greens or romaine lettuce and fill these with my favorite foods. You can also use nori, which is a type of seaweed that comes in sheets, as a wrap. We discussed bread in the previous chapter, but it is worth mentioning again; if you choose to eat bread, make sure it is made from sprouted whole organic grains and not just whole wheat. There's a big difference between the two. Look for sprouted and check the label; it has a much greater nutritional value. If you do eat bread, toast it before you make your sandwich. Toasting grains helps break down the gluten in the flour and makes the bread easier to digest.

Lunch should be a really great meal and one to enjoy. I prefer a hot lunch, but that is not everyone's choice so do what works for you. There are so many different choices for lunch and you can have whatever you want as long as you follow the rule of 'real foods, whole foods.' Read the labels and buy food with the least amount of ingredients possible, as well as ones that you can actually pronounce and understand what they are. Be creative with spices, and use them abundantly.

I also like to tell my clients to stay away from drinking fluids during their meals. The reason for this is that our stomachs have something called hydrochloric acid, and that acid can burn through almost anything. It is such a powerful acid, and it is there to help us digest our food. We need it to be at its maximum strength for digestion and that will not happen if it is watered down. If we drink too much during our meal, the acid becomes less potent and less capable of breaking down the food in our stomachs. So, try to avoid drinking during your meals. If you need a sip of water because your mouth is dry, then by all means have it; but don't gulp large amounts of fluid. Wait a half an hour to drink after your meal, and stop drinking fluids a half hour prior to your meal. Enjoy your lunch and have lots of vegetables, leafy greens and protein. Remember to drink lots of water between meals.

Twelve

TIME FOR DINNER

"It's not the will to win that matters – everyone has that. It's the will to prepare to win that matters."

-PAUL BRYANT, FOOTBALL COACH

Dinner should be the lightest meal of your day. It should be consumed by 7 p.m. to give your body the maximum amount of time to digest before going to sleep. Unfortunately, most people do the complete opposite and make dinner their largest meal. Most people eat their dinners way too late, as well. When this happens, sleep is usually interrupted and not sound. How many of us have gone out to dinner late, consumed way too much food, and lain in bed bloated and uncomfortable—unable to sleep? Try to eat earlier and consume less food.

There are many good choices for a light meal; try soups and steamed vegetables. If you're going to have animal protein, keep it to a small amount and make sure it is consumed early in the evening; animal protein takes a much longer time to digest. Avoid sweets at night because they too will affect your ability to sleep. After dinner is finished, it's a good idea to completely shut down the kitchen and consider all food off limits. Most people tell me they have no problems consuming the right foods during the day, but totally lose that ability in the late afternoon and after dinner. This is when the majority of snacking occurs; most of the time this is a direct result of not eating complete, balanced meals for breakfast and lunch. When we do not fuel correctly, the body starts searching for the nutrients it did not receive at those meals. If you are an after dinner nosher, try to replace that habit with some other activity or make yourself a cup of peppermint or chamomile tea and sip it slowly.

Thirteen

HOW AND WHERE WE EAT

"When you're in a rut, you have to question everything except your ability to get out of it."

-*TWYLA THARP, CHOREOGRAPHER*

E ating is a sacred ritual, and should be honored as such. We all need to make the time in our busy lives to sit down and eat our meals. This means that you must plan ahead and have your food ready, or at least available, when mealtime arrives. If you have no time in the morning to eat breakfast, then I would advise you to set your alarm clock at least 20 minutes earlier. For moms who are busy getting their children off to school, this is very important. If you can get up before your children do and eat your breakfast, it will make your morning run a lot smoother. This will also stop you from picking leftovers off your children's plates and eating your breakfast in the car as you drive them to school. If you are someone who doesn't like to eat before their morning workout, I suggest you have a protein shake prior to exercising. A shake can be prepared quickly and give you that extra boost while training. Please do not eat your breakfast or any meal while driving in your car! For starters it is way too distracting, and also not at all good for digestion. In order for you to digest your food properly and absorb all the nutrients, food must be eaten while your body is at rest and without stress. We all know driving can be stressful and traffic is not a peaceful environment.

Lunch and dinner should also be eaten in a peaceful environment, and hopefully in a resting state. I suggest you shut off your computer, and if you are watching TV, turn it off. Sit quietly and take a moment to appreciate and acknowledge the food on your plate. Observe the colors of your food, the aroma it gives off. Right before you begin to eat, take a moment and give thanks for the food you're about to eat. Practice mindful eating. Chew your food well, and eat slowly. A lot of times we eat really quickly and do not properly chew our food. All foods should be chewed until they become liquefied. The reason for this is because digestion begins in the mouth. Our saliva is loaded with digestive enzymes, which helps break down the food and prepares it for digestion. When we gulp down our food without properly chewing it, we miss a very important first step in breaking down our food. Eating too quickly without chewing also leads to overeating. By the time our brain gets the message that we are full, we have already overeaten. Take it slowly and chew your food. Put your fork down in between bites. If that doesn't help, use chopsticks. The slower and more relaxed you are while eating, the better you will digest your food. You will consume less food, resulting in fewer calories and reduce the chances of overeating.

So many Americans suffer from IBS and other digestive concerns, that it would be wise to re-evaluate how and when we eat. Take the time to go grocery shopping and have the food you need available. Organization and planning play a critical role in being able to supply your body with nourishing food. Make it a priority, and you will drastically improve the quality of your life. "IF NOT NOW, WHEN?"

Fourteen

"Someone much smarter than me once said,
"Don't go with the flow. You are the flow."

- *MEREDITH VIEIRA, JOURNALIST*

Another great way to bring energy and vitality to your life is through a process known as earthing. Some may be more familiar with the term grounding. Grounding is when you walk barefoot on the earth or sit down and make contact with the earth somewhere on your body. Our bodies are loaded with inflammation, and that inflammation is the cause of many chronic diseases. Illnesses such as heart disease, diabetes, and arthritis are diseases involving inflammation. One of the ways that we can reduce our bodies' inflammation is through the process of grounding.

Think of the earth as a very large battery, one which has a negative charge. The problem with humans is that we are much more likely to have a positive charge, and this is what causes the inflammation. We receive all these positive charges through the use of cell phones, computers, TVs, and all the objects around us with strong electric magnetic fields called EMFs. These EMFs are bombarding our bodies with positive charges, and these are adding to the inflammation of our bodies. From the beginning of time when man first appeared on this earth, he walked barefooted and was connected to the pull of the earth's core. This allowed for a constant connection to the earth's powerful magnetic field. This pull has the ability to rid the body of any positive charges, and by doing so helps to keep the body in a neutral state, with very little inflammation. It works very much like a giant cleanse detoxifying the body of EMFs.

It's so easy to ground yourself, and it's free. All you need to do is take your shoes off and walk barefoot. You can connect with the earth through the grass, rock, dirt, and water; you cannot ground yourself through asphalt and concrete. The connection must be with the surface of the earth. Water is a great conductor of that negative charge; when you go out into a body of water you can actually feel the difference in energy fields. So many people tell me they have the most energy and get sick less often in the warm summer months. I believe it is because we build a very strong immune system by ridding our bodies of all the EMFs' positive charge, either by walking barefoot or swimming in a body of water. If you're fortunate enough to get to swim in an ocean, a lake, or a river you will feel the enormous healing powers that water possesses.

When we are stuck inside all through the cold winter months, how can we take advantage of the benefits of grounding? We obviously cannot go barefoot outside, so how do we ground ourselves? There are many products sold today that can help us ground, even if you live in a high-rise apartment building and it's winter time. Google earthing or grounding pads and check out all your different options. I myself use both grounding pads and bedding. Check them out; it's well worth it.

"IF NOT NOW, WHEN?"

Fifteen

Stop the Excuses and Start Moving

*"You miss a hundred percent of
the shots you don't take."*

-Wayne Gretzky, hockey player

A big part of exercise is just doing it. I ask my clients all the time, "What are you waiting for—a better day, more time, when you're feeling better?" I hear people quite frequently saying, "When I lose some weight, I'll start exercising." Isn't that the point of coming to a fitness studio in the first place, to lose weight? Another frequently used excuse is, "I'm just too busy right now. When things slow down, I'll be there."

There is never a great or perfect time to start any of this, but you just have to start, because life will get in the way no matter what. If you do not schedule your exercise like you schedule everything else in your life, you will never do it. If you want to get it done, you have to make it a habit like brushing your teeth. It cannot be the first thing you forfeit when another obligation pulls at you. Everything you need to get done must be scheduled around your exercise. You have to make it a priority in your day. Soon it will become a habit, one that is so ingrained you don't ever think about not doing it.

This is so important for your health and well-being. It will help build the energy you need to live a very full life, a life where you can accomplish many things because you have an abundance of energy. Exercise gives you the ability to build energy, to become stronger and thus healthier. There is no doubt that health and exercise have a direct link to each other. Exercise brings blood and oxygen to all the muscles, ligaments, and organs in your body. I always say, "A good sweat is better than any facial." When you sweat, you're detoxifying and cleansing your whole body; it's so good for you. After you work up a sweat, it is a good idea to take a shower as soon as possible so you don't reabsorb all the toxins that your body released. The best detoxifier is a good sweat.

How do we start, and what is the best form of exercise to begin with? All movement is good, and each individual must look to what they will enjoy. If you don't enjoy it, you will not stick with it. If you haven't worked out in a very long time and are overweight, start slow. Walking is a fantastic way to begin exercising if you are overweight. It is very hard on your body to start jogging, spinning, or kickboxing if there is too much weight on your body, because it will create too much stress on your joints and ligaments. First, begin with your diet and you'll start losing weight. Add to that a brisk walk and things will really begin to shift in your body. You do not have to do any more than that and the weight will begin to come off. Unfortunately, a lot of people who decide to lose weight set their expectations way too high, which will make those goals almost impossible to achieve. I say, "Start slow with realistic goals." Go outside and walk at a pace that is challenging to you; it can't be a leisurely stroll—you have to feel the effort. It does not have to be so fast that you are running, and no, it doesn't have to be painful. But, you do have to feel the work.

Sixteen

"Ninety–nine percent of all failures come from people who have a habit of making excuses."

-George Washington Carver, scientist

I suggest that everyone should wear a heart rate monitor and keep a record of their heart rate to track health improvement. Keeping this record is a wonderful way to look back and see where your heart rate was and where it is now. As you become stronger, the heart rate will drop. A good example of this is when someone new to exercising takes a spin class and does a sprint which causes their heart rate to rise into the 180s. When a heart rate goes up that high, it means the heart is beating extremely quickly to get the blood and oxygen circulating to where it is needed. As you build your aerobic base and the strength of your heart, which is a muscle, you will become stronger. After training for a while, you will notice that your heart rate will begin to drop in those sprints; instead of your heart rate beating at 180 beats per minute, it may stay at 150 beats per minute. What that means is, instead of your heart beating so quickly to pump the blood to your muscles, you have built up the strength of both your heart and lungs so they can work much more efficiently. One good pump pushes out much more blood, instead of needing to pump many times to get the same blood flow. So start slow and build a strong aerobic base.

There are many charts out there that will help guide you as to what your heart rate should be at 75%, 80%, 85%, and threshold. A lot of them go by your age, weight, and physical activity level. You can easily research this and find out what your heart rate zones are. Keeping the heart rates lower rather than higher during a hard workout is always better. I know you cardio junkies out there love to go fast and furious and get those heart rates up to maximum. At these high heart rates, you have sent your body into what is called an anaerobic state. In this state your body is burning sugar for fuel, not fat. Yes, this is good to do once in a while, but it isn't something you want to be doing every day or every time you do cardio, because it's extremely stressful on the body. If you're doing that on a continuous basis, all of these wonderful benefits you get from exercise start to switch and what was once great for you begins to break down your muscles and body strength instead of building them. Be really conscious of that next time you do cardio, and remember you don't need to go fast and furious every time you work out. Instead, try to keep the heart rate down in what is called the endurance zone or the aerobic zone. This is the zone of a marathon runner; he never goes anaerobic.

Anaerobic is very stressful on the body. You want to try to keep an aerobic phase where you will be utilizing fat for fuel, not sugar. This is why a lot of people who finish an intense cardio workout, and have continuously taken their heart rate into the anaerobic zone, are either exhausted or they want to eat a house when they are finished. They are craving simple carbohydrates or sugar. Carbohydrates convert to glucose in the body and the body runs on glucose. The body needs it for bursts of energy, but it doesn't need high quantities of it; AND CERTAINLY NOT IN THE FORM OF BREAD. Let's burn more fat than sugar for fuel and lower our body fat index by staying in an aerobic zone.

Once you have placed your heart rate monitor on and you can see your heart rate going up into those high numbers, your breathing will get heavy. This is an indicator that you have entered into the anaerobic zone. That anaerobic zone is like a light switch in your body. Once you turn it on, it stays on. You cannot turn it off and go back into the aerobic zone. Even if you drop your heart rate, your body will stay in that anaerobic zone until you have finished your workout. Be aware of this next time you go take a class. I'm a big believer in heart rate monitors. They will help you become aware of your heart rate zones, which will help you build stronger bodies and reduce body fat. In the long run you will wind up with more energy and less stress, and you will not feel exhausted after taking a class. You will build a strong aerobic base, a strong foundation; and like we discussed earlier in this chapter, you're going to make that heart beat more efficiently, empowering the whole body.

It is important to remember that stress hormones are stress hormones, no matter how they occur. If we lose our luggage in the airport or we are sending our heart rates into the anaerobic zone during a cardio class, the stress hormones are exactly the same. Sure, you enjoy the cardio class more, but that doesn't change the fact you are still releasing stress hormones. Repeatedly releasing that many stress hormones in the body will eventually break down the body. Don't misunderstand me. I am not saying that you should never take it to those high heart rate levels—just not every single time.

For many people, the need to exercise every day can become an addiction, and not necessarily a healthy one. They can become exercise junkies and push themselves regardless of whether they are tired or not feeling well; this is the opposite of healthy. When you exercise regardless of how you are feeling because you feel guilty if you don't, that is just as bad as someone who never exercises. It is important to understand the balance. If you feel you have to exercise hard, no matter what, you are totally out of balance and you do not get the yin and yang of it. You cannot always go hard. You also need to visit the softer side of exercise. When we are out of balance in body and mind, illness and injury will follow. If you are someone who wakes up in the morning—and you are not feeling well, but you push yourself anyway—that's a big mistake.

Honor your body. That's the number one, most important thing. Pay attention to the signals it sends you; be aware of them and listen. The body is brilliant and it talks to you. But if you put earmuffs and blinders on, and you don't pay attention, the body starts to talk to you louder as time goes on. In the beginning, the body might just start tapping you a little. Maybe it's just a little twinge in your knee; this is the way the body is telling you to pay attention, but you don't and you continue to run and exercise on that leg. The tap becomes a little stronger and still you ignore it. Now it becomes a bit stronger; and if you still pay no attention to the nagging twinges and aches, eventually the body will punch you and you'll have to take notice. This may come in the form of a torn muscle or a bad sprain; whatever it is, it's a direct result of you not paying attention to the signals your body was sending you. So remember this every time you push yourself when you are not feeling great. I'm not talking about taking the easy way out, or making excuses just because you may not feel like exercising. That's a whole other issue. I'm talking about abusing yourself and your incredible body; there is a big difference between the two.

Movement is healing to the body, if done correctly. Not only does it bring oxygen to all the cells in your body and build that strong heart, it also makes you feel good. It affects your mood, your attitude, how you feel about your day and your life. This is especially important for people who suffer from depression and or anxiety. Getting out and just moving your body will cause so much anxiety to dissipate, because it releases what I call the 'happy hormones'—the endorphins that make you feel great. Again, it's all about balance.

What is balance? If you're going to do a hard cardio one day, then the next day you should do a pilates or yoga class where you focus on strengthening and toning. These type of classes will help to restore the balance of your body. And just because you are not going anaerobic during these workouts does not mean they are not intense workouts. It's just different, and different is good. If you do the softer exercise one day, do your kickboxing or your spin class the next day. This way the body gets both types of workout, and you help to balance your body and brain. This is really key to keeping a healthy well-balanced body.

Seventeen

USE IT OR LOSE IT

"The first step towards getting somewhere is to decide that you are not going to stay where you are."

-J.P. MORGAN, FINANCIER

⟵⟶

The other thing I would like to discuss is the way modern technology has changed movement for us, and it's a little scary to tell you the truth. I don't think most people are aware of what's going on, but it really disturbs me when I see what's happening in our society and the world around us. Years ago when you went to an airport, you would have to lift your luggage. And by doing so, you would engage the muscles of your arms, legs, back, and core. Now everything is on wheels, and we no longer use those muscles as much. This is another step backwards in our fitness levels. By adding those wheels, we have taken away another aspect of our fitness training. That's just the beginning of the problem. Not only do we not have to lift our luggage anymore, we don't have to walk either. The airports have installed moveable floors. God forbid we have to use our legs!

I don't know about you, but I find this extremely disturbing. If you don't use them, you will lose them. I always make a joke that through evolution, the generations to come are going to be born with tails and giant thumbs. Giant thumbs because all everyone does is text, text, text; tails because no one wants to walk anywhere anymore. Everyone is driving and sitting. What are we doing to our bodies and our health when we take away the body's natural movement patterns? What about escalators? There are places now where you can't even find a flight of stairs, and you are forced to use escalators. That angers me; yes, I know you can walk up an escalator, but it's a lot easier than walking up a flight of stairs. Every time I have a choice between the two, I take the stairs. My family is always making fun of me saying things like, "Where is mom? Oh yeah, she's on the stairs again." But it's funny how things work out. When my children were younger they always chose the escalators, but as they got older they started taking the stairs too. You influence the people around you. Lead by example and always take the stairs.

I also find it amazing that there are people who will take three hours of classes in the gym, hammering it out; but when they get in their cars, they will drive 10 to 15 minutes in the shopping center to find a parking space up front. How bizarre is that? If you can work out for three hours in the morning, you'd think you would be able to walk across a parking lot to get to the store. Gyms were meant as a convenience because we can't always get outside to exercise. I look at a gym as a place to train—so that when I leave the gym and go out and live my life, I can do it with strength, endurance, and power. We need that strength so we can do things in our daily lives, such as lifting that 5-gallon water jug and placing it in the dispenser; we need to put that training to good use.

Another good form of functional training is shoveling snow. There have been days where I had to close my studio due to a snowstorm and clients would be asking me, "What will I do for exercise?" My answer is, "Get outside and shovel." It's a great combination of everything we do in the gym; here's your squat, your lunges, and your twists. You are also activating your core, your obliques; it's all there in shoveling. If you can't shovel, but you can work out for two hours in a row at the gym, there's a problem in how you are training.

How about those electric fences? How many people actually walk their dogs anymore? Put your dog on a leash and take your dog for a walk. The best companion on a walk is a dog; they don't argue with you, they're as happy as can be, they don't talk, and you can actually enjoy your walk. So get out there and walk your dog. It's great exercise. Long Island has so many beautiful parks and beaches—great places to walk. We drive everywhere, get out, and start walking. So many people spend their time at the gyms taking spin classes day in and day out, and most of those spinners have never been on a real road bike or off-road bike. Isn't that the point, so you can eventually get outside and ride your bike in the great outdoors and have fun doing it?

Train smart, healthy, with balance, and pay attention to your body. Look and listen for signs of distress. Start with any kind of movement, whatever you like, but move, there are no excuses. If not now when, what are you waiting for? You don't have to start big; start small and build up your fitness level. I guarantee if you do too much too fast, you will either get injured or you will stop out of frustration. The body has to start slow; you can't run before you walk. So start slow and get moving. There's no excuse for not moving your body. I don't care how busy you are in your life, move it or you will lose it. As you age, you will find that your body loses strength and endurance. The only way to keep it strong is with exercise. Get out there and move if you want beautiful skin, beautiful hair, an abundance of energy, and great muscle tone.

People are always talking about how exhausted they are. My question is, "How much exercise have you done today?" It can go both ways; you can over-exercise and be exhausted because you overdid it, or you may not move your body at all and be exhausted. You have to find a balance. Everything we discuss in this book is about finding the balance, what works for you. "IF NOT NOW WHEN?"

Eighteen

THE NEED TO BE CONNECTED

*"There is a purpose to our lives, even if it is
sometimes hidden from us, and even if the biggest
turning points and heartbreaks only make sense
as we look back, not as we are experiencing them.
So we might as well live life as if, as the poet
Rumi put it, "Everything is rigged in our favor."*

-ARIANNA HUFFINGTON, MEDIA MOGUEL

There is a constant need in our society to feel (and be) connected. It's a response that sometimes makes people feel
left out and alone. I believe that we need to reconnect with
ourselves and spend more time disconnected from the world,
so we can connect to what really matters.

This type of disconnecting is very freeing. This is the feeling I have when I leave my cell phone behind. I realize that we all have families and commitments, but do we constantly have to be checking those phones for messages? The bottom line is, someone is always going to need you for something. I raised my oldest daughter without the use of a cell phone and I raised my youngest one with one, and I have to say life was much calmer without a cell phone. If my oldest daughter needed me, she always knew where I was and would reach out if it was important. She didn't call me for every little thing. The problem today is people do not know how to live without a phone connected to them at all times; they never put them away. Can you imagine going in for a massage and bringing your cell phone with you, or going into a group meditation and not leaving that phone behind, and during that time the phone rings? I have seen this happen more often than I would like to acknowledge. How about taking that hour for yourself during spin class or at the gym without the distraction of cell phones? Believe me, if it's an emergency you will be found! I've noticed that the majority of the texts and phone calls we receive are from people requesting something from us and by doing so, they are putting more stress and demands upon our precious time.

I love the days when I leave my cell phone either in the car or at home and no one can reach me for a period of time. It is very freeing! How many of you have tried this? When you do eventually get to your phone, it has 20 missed texts and a bunch of missed calls on it, and all of those people expect you to call or text them back; it's exhausting!!! I tell my friends and my family that I do not carry the phone with me everywhere I go, so please excuse me if I do not respond immediately. By doing this, I allow myself to be completely in the moment and focused on the here and now. I will eventually go through those messages, but I will do it when I decide to spend that time and focus on them.

How many of us are practicing awareness when we are speaking on the phone? How many times are you picking up your children from school or driving them somewhere—and talking on the phone while they are trying to tell you something? You are listening with half an ear, and they know it. Maybe you are spending time together, but you keep answering your text messages instead of paying attention to them. It would be much better for everyone if the phone was put away and you could give your children your undivided attention; you could actually listen to what they had to say. If you want your children to confide in you and ask your opinion on things, you have to make the effort to pay full attention and be present when they try to talk to you; otherwise they will stop trying.

Texting has taken the human element out of connecting with each other. What happened to speaking with each other in person, or calling each other and hearing a voice on the other end? When you speak to someone, you can hear the tone and emotion in their voice—something that is totally lost in texting. Texting has become the method of choice for so many, yet isn't it a cop out in many ways? What if you have to explain something you've done or something you are going to do and it's an uncomfortable subject? Isn't it easier to text someone then to actually confront the situation in person or over the phone? Texting is the easy way out, because you don't have to feel or see their emotions; you're able to screen their questions before answering them.

One of my rules for my children when they were still in high school and driving cars to friends' houses is that they had to call me and speak directly to me. They were not allowed to text me to say that they were okay, because I wanted to hear their voices and the noise in the background. I made my children own up to where they were and what they were doing. I knew they couldn't fool me when I could hear their voices, something a text message does not provide.

Bullying and cyber bullying are big problems today. It's so easy to hurt people when you're not face to face and not looking into someone's eyes, but you're hiding behind a computer or a text message. By doing this, we don't have to take responsibility for our actions and see the pain we may have caused in someone else's eyes. Let us all be fully aware that the human connection is removed in the cyber world, the connection of our spirits and our souls are not felt through a text message. A text message is great for a quick little message, but not for something important you need to say. It stunts our emotional development and hinders our ability to socialize. When you are in a tough situation or you're in a fight with someone, either they've hurt you or you've hurt them, you need to confront that person face to face. You need to look into their eyes and see their body language; here is where you grow—both in your ability to communicate and to empathize. We will learn so much more about how to handle ourselves and our own emotions when confronted this way, than we could ever learn from a text message or Facebook.

Texting can enable us and our children in many ways. If you have young children they might text you saying, "Hey mom, can you bring me my homework or my lunch because I forgot it?" However, if they are texting you all day asking you if can you do this and can you do that, and you constantly respond, over time this will not help them. If they do not take responsibility for remembering their homework or anything else, and they know that they can just text you and you will take care of it for them, they will never take responsibility for themselves. If you jump, no matter what you are doing, you are teaching them that your time does not matter—and they will lose respect for both you and your time. Be careful of falling into this pattern with both your family and friends. We need to teach our children that our time is valuable and should be respected, unless we want to create children who grow up expecting people to do everything for them without taking the responsibility to manage their own lives.

I recently had lunch with an old friend that I was really looking forward to seeing and catching up with what was going on in her life. The whole time we were at that table, she had her phone connected to her, checking her emails and looking at her text messages. Every time someone texted her she would say, "Excuse me I just have to answer this." I felt very disconnected, a little insulted, and it made me feel insignificant. Anyone who has ever felt insignificant knows it doesn't feel very good. I was sitting there thinking about how I had to rearrange my whole schedule to be at this lunch. I wanted to be in the moment and present for my friend, and I was expecting her to do the same. It was really sad that she could not disconnect herself for the hour it would have taken us to have lunch and be present with each other. She couldn't enjoy the conversation, the food, nothing, all because she wasn't in the moment. She looked so stressed; this is exactly what I am talking about with my clients when I talk about creating your own madness and stress.

Life is already very stressful, with so many demands placed on us. Why create more by constantly feeling the need to carry our phones everywhere we go and answer all those messages? Why are we adding more stress to what already exists in our lives? Granted, I think texting, Facebook and all the social media that is available today are wonderful tools, but I think we are misusing them. I think these tools are actually using us; that is where I feel lines need to be drawn and decisions have to be made. You need to place value on your time and space. Has texting become another addiction for us to deal with? Ask yourself how many times a day are you checking that phone and what would happen if you left that phone behind. Would that make you crazy? Are the majority of the texts you receive in a day that important, and are the constant interruptions of your life worth it? Do they interrupt your enjoyment, flow, and patterns? Regarding the people you could be spending time with, are you half in the moment and half out? Are you texting while you are driving, or lost in a conversation on your phone while you are behind that wheel? The use of these tools should improve our lives, not make them more stressful and danger-ous. Think about that, next time you reach for that phone!!

In Conclusion

I hope in reading this book you will have learned a few important ways to access some of that power which lies within each and every one of us. It is a place where we are ageless and vibrant, with an abundance of joy and energy. One of the ways we can achieve all of this is by simply being kind to ourselves and loving ourselves unconditionally. Own your own power, and remember that power begins with you and how you treat your body and spirit.

Laugh more, love more and smile more; practice smiling at others and watch how your day unfolds if you start it with a smile. When you're smiling, as the saying goes, "THE WHOLE WORLD SMILES WITH YOU." Think about the face you show to others, the energy you give off, because that will be the energy you create for yourself and everyone around you. If a problem confronts you, try not to see it as happening to you but instead, happening for you; it's pushing you to choose a different path, one that you may be fearful of—but one that just might transform your life!

When all is said and done, you came into this world all by yourself and you will leave this place all by yourself; so remember to be your own best friend. And as that friend—honor, respect, and love yourself.

Peace and love to you all,

Ellen

Acknowledgements

I would like to thank my beautiful family for all their love and support. I cherish every moment that we spend together, preparing amazing food with love and laughter. For all our lively conversations about food, around food and with food, we have spent as much time discussing food as we have eating it! I truly believe food nurtures not only our bodies, but our souls as well.

To my husband Steve, for always supporting and encouraging me, no matter how crazy my ideas are, and for helping me develop my voice and showing me what true self-confidence really is.

To my three incredible children: Lauren, Sean and Hannah. Lauren, for keeping my feet on the ground when I begin to float away. Sean, for your wonderful sense of humor, and the push you gave me to get it done. "IF NOT NOW, WHEN?" Hannah, for the pride I see in your eyes when you look at me.

I love you all, you are my greatest source of inspiration and joy.

To all my teachers and mentors along the way who have dedicated their lives to the quest for health and wellness. Without all of you, none of this would be possible.

To my Shihan and friend, John Busto, for teaching me the art of patience.

To my brilliant trainer, John Diflorio, for never allowing me to get away with one less rep!!!

To the amazing front desk staff at Rock Pilates. To my manager, Brittany, for believing in my dream and doing all the jobs needed to run Rock Pilates, thus allowing me the time and space I need to create.

To all the instructors at Rock Pilates for their devotion and support. To all the amazing clients I have had the privilege to know over the years; all of you have taught me lessons about the human spirit that are invaluable.

About the Author

Ellen Nalaboff has been part of the wellness industry for twenty-five years. Through her knowledge and expertise, she has helped thousands of people take charge of their lives—including many well-known celebrities, CEOs, and public figures.

Ellen holds numerous degrees in health, nutrition, and fitness. She is certified in classical Pilates and spinning and holds a black belt in Kenpo karate. Board –certified by the American Association of Drugless Practitioners and the C.H.E.K. institute in California as a Holistic Health Counselor and Life Coach with accreditations from Colombia University Teachers College. Ellen is also one of 800 global instructors chosen by Deepak Chopra to teach Primordial Sound Meditation.

She is the founder and owner of ROCK PILATES, where Ellen aims to strengthen the mind by nourishing the body and spirit. She encourages laughter and acceptance while building a community of friends in pursuit of a healthy, balanced, and harmonious life.